# When Your Heart Needs Healing

Scriptures for the Heart- Book 1

Cindy August

Creative Books Plus Publishing

ISBN: Paperback: 9781970947076

For permissions, inquiries, or bulk orders, visit:
www.creativebooksplus.net

# Contents

# Dedication

To the one who feels forgotten, unseen, or overwhelmed...
this book is for you.

May every page remind you that God has never left you,
never stopped loving you,
and never stopped holding your heart.

May His healing reach the places no one else can see,
and may joy return to you in a way that only He can restore.

With all my heart,
**Cindy August**

# Acknowledgements

I want to thank my Heavenly Father, whose love continues to heal the deepest parts of my heart.

To Jesus, my Savior and Shepherd —
every scripture in this book points back to Your faithfulness.

To the Holy Spirit —
thank You for guiding every word, every chapter, and every breath of this project. Your presence is the true Comforter in every heart that will read these pages.

To my family, friends, and church community —
thank you for your prayers, your encouragement, and your love.

And to every reader holding this book right now —
you are not alone.
You are so deeply loved by God.
And I pray these pages wrap your heart in His presence, peace, and healing.

# Introduction

There are seasons in life that leave us feeling fragile —
moments when sorrow is heavy,
when loneliness settles deep,
when our hearts ache in ways we can't fully explain.

This book was created for those seasons.

*When Your Heart Needs Healing* is the first in the *Scriptures for the Heart* series —
a collection designed to gently guide you from:

hurt → healing → hope → joy.

You will find:

One primary scripture in each chapter

Supporting verses that breathe truth and comfort

A "Comfort for the Heart" reflection to lift your spirit

A steady progression from pain to God's healing presence

This is not a book of quick fixes or clichés.
This is a journey with God —
the God who sees your tears,

hears your prayers,
and holds your heart with tender love.

As you read these chapters, may you sense:

His nearness

His comfort

His strength

His goodness

His joy returning to you

You don't have to rush through this.
Let each chapter speak to your heart in its own time.
Let the Word wash over you.
Let God meet you right where you are.

My prayer is simple:

**May this book become a quiet place of healing, a gentle companion on hard days, and a reminder that your heart is safe in God's hands.**

Let's begin this journey —
together.

With love,
**Cindy August**

# Series Note

**About the *Scriptures for the Heart* Series — Book 1**

*When Your Heart Needs Healing*

*Scriptures for the Heart* was created to gently meet readers in their pain and lead them toward hope through the healing power of God's Word.

Each book in this series focuses on a specific emotional and spiritual need, offering:
• Carefully chosen Bible verses
• Gentle reassurance for wounded hearts
• A clear progression from pain to healing
• God's promises arranged with compassion and purpose

**Book 1** speaks directly to the brokenhearted.
It was written for those walking through grief, loneliness, abandonment, heartbreak, trauma, or deep emotional sorrow. If your heart feels heavy, fragile, or overwhelmed, these pages are meant to remind you that God is near, attentive, and tenderly involved in your healing.

This book does not rush the pain or minimize the hurt. Instead, it allows space for honesty while steadily guiding the heart from sorrow to comfort, from despair to hope, and ultimately toward renewed joy.

May these Scriptures wrap your heart in God's presence and gently remind you that even in brokenness, you are deeply loved — and healing is already underway.

# Section 1

## WHEN PAIN FEELS HEAVY

There are moments when pain feels too deep for words. This section allows you to acknowledge the hurt, to breathe, and to know that God sees every part of your heart.

# CHAPTER 1

# WHEN YOUR HEART FEELS BROKEN

**Psalm 34:18**

*"The Lord is near to those who have a broken heart, And saves such as have a contrite spirit."*

**Psalm 147:3**

*"He heals the brokenhearted, And binds up their wounds."*

**Isaiah 61:1**

*"He has sent Me to heal the brokenhearted..."*

**Psalm 73:26**

*"My flesh and my heart fail; But God is the strength of my heart and my portion forever."*

**Psalm 55:22**

*"Cast your burden on the Lord, And He shall sustain you; He shall never permit the righteous to be moved."*

## COMFORT FOR THE HEART

There are moments when the weight of a broken heart feels too heavy to describe. But the Scriptures you just read whisper a truth that grief tries to hide:

**You are not alone in this pain — God is right here.**

The world may not see the cracks in your heart. People may not understand the depth of what you're carrying. But God does.
And He isn't standing far off, waiting for you to "be strong." He draws near to the wounded, the weary, and those fighting to hold themselves together.

His nearness is not just a promise — It is His character. He comes close to comfort. He comes close to bind up wounds. He comes close to breathe peace where sorrow has taken your air.

The verses in this chapter reveal a God who:

Stays close to the brokenhearted

Heals what feels impossible to repair

Strengthens the heart when it feels like it's failing

Replaces troubled thoughts with His peace

Carries what you were never meant to lift alone

Your heart breaks, but His heart bends toward you. Your strength may fade, but His never will.

Rest in this today: **God is not just aware of your pain — He is actively healing it.** Right now, even in this very moment, He is binding wounds you cannot see and lifting burdens you've held for far too long.

Let these Scriptures be a soft place for your heart to land. He is near. He is gentle. He is healing you — one breath, one moment, one touch at a time.

# Chapter 2

# When Grief Overwhelms You

**Matthew 5:4**

*"Blessed are those who mourn, For they shall be comforted."*

**Psalm 30:5**

*"Weeping may endure for a night, But joy comes in the morning."*

**Isaiah 41:10**

*"Fear not, for I am with you; Be not dismayed, for I am your God. I will strengthen you, Yes, I will help you, I will uphold you with My righteous right hand."*

**Revelation 21:4**

*"And God will wipe away every tear from their eyes; there shall be no more death, nor sorrow, nor crying."*

**Psalm 56:8**

*"You number my wanderings; Put my tears into Your bottle; Are they not in Your book?"*

## COMFORT FOR THE HEART

Grief can feel like a tidal wave— rising without warning, knocking the breath out of you, leaving you unsure of how to stand again. But the Scriptures you just read reveal something breathtaking:

**God does not meet you after the storm... He meets you *in* it.**

Jesus Himself promised comfort to those who mourn. Not judgment. Not pressure. Not a quick command to "be strong." But *comfort* — deep, personal, supernatural comfort.

Grief is not a sign of weak faith. It is a sign that love existed. And the God who gave you that love now gathers your tears with His own hands.

The verses in this chapter remind your heart that: God sees every tear, He counts every sorrow, He walks the long road of healing with you, His compassion never runs out, He has already prepared a future without pain, Your grief is not invisible to Heaven. It is held, honored, and answered with divine compassion.

When grief feels overwhelming, remember this:

**God is not asking you to rush your healing — He is offering to carry you through it.**

Let His promises wrap around you like a warm blanket on a cold night. Let His nearness steady your trembling heart. Let His faithfulness remind you that morning always follows the night.

Joy will return.
Peace will return.
Strength will return.

But for now, God is simply holding you —
and that is enough.

# CHAPTER 3

# WHEN TRAUMA STILL ECHOES INSIDE

**Psalm 147:3**

*"He heals the brokenhearted, and binds up their wounds."*

**Isaiah 43:2**

*"When you pass through the waters, I will be with you; and through the rivers, they shall not overflow you..."*

**Psalm 34:4**

*"I sought the Lord, and He heard me, and delivered me from all my fears."*

**Joel 2:25**

*"So I will restore to you the years that the swarming locust has eaten..."*

**2 Corinthians 1:3–4**

*"The Father of mercies and God of all comfort, who comforts us in all our tribulation..."*

## COMFORT FOR THE HEART

Trauma has a way of echoing long after the moment has passed. A sound, a memory, a phrase, a place — and suddenly the heart tightens, the mind races, the past feels painfully present again.

But hear this clearly:

**God does not dismiss the wounds you carry.**
**He heals them. Tenderly. Faithfully. Thoroughly.**

The Scriptures you just read tell the story of a God who: walks with you through deep waters, listens when fear rises, restores what was stolen, comforts you in places no one else can reach, strengthens you when you feel fragile inside.

Trauma tries to convince you that you're alone, that healing is impossible, that you'll never feel whole again.

But trauma does not get the final word —
**God does.**

And His word is:

**"I am with you." "I will deliver you." "I will restore you."**
**"I will bind your wounds." "I know you."**

You are not too broken for Him. You are not too complicated for Him. You are not too wounded for Him.

Your trauma may echo, but His comfort speaks louder. And where His voice enters, healing begins.

Let Him wrap His peace around the parts of you that still tremble. Let Him step into the memories that feel heavy. Let Him turn the echo of your trauma into the echo of His love.

Healing is happening — slowly, gently, beautifully. One layer at a time. One breath at a time. One whisper of His presence at a time.

# Chapter 4

# When Loneliness Feels Endless

**Deuteronomy 31:8**

*"And the Lord, He is the One who goes before you. He will be with you, He will not leave you nor forsake you; do not fear nor be dismayed."*

**Isaiah 41:13**

*"For I, the Lord your God, will hold your right hand, Saying to you, 'Fear not, I will help you.'"*

**Hebrews 13:5**

*"For He Himself has said, 'I will never leave you nor forsake you.'"*

**Psalm 25:16**

*"Turn Yourself to me, and have mercy on me, For I am desolate and afflicted."*

**John 14:18**

*"I will not leave you orphans; I will come to you."*

## COMFORT FOR THE HEART

Loneliness isn't just the absence of people — it is the ache of feeling unseen, unheard, or uncared for. It can hit you in a crowded room, in a marriage, in a family, or in seasons where everyone seems to have a place but you. But the Scriptures you just read remind you of a truth deeper than the ache:

**You are never actually alone. Not for one moment. Not for one breath.**

God Himself promises over and over again:

***"I am with you. I will hold your hand. I will not abandon you. I will come to you. I will take care of you.***

Loneliness tries to tell you that you've been forgotten. God tells you that you are deeply remembered. Loneliness whispers that no one sees you. God declares that He sees *every* detail of your heart. Loneliness says the emptiness will last forever. God says He goes before you, beside you, and behind you.

Even when people fail, even when relationships shift, even when seasons change —

**God's presence stays. God's love stays. God's care stays.**

He sits with you in the quiet. He stands with you in the storm. He walks with you through every empty hallway of life. Your loneliness is not a sign that God is far away — it is an opportunity to feel His nearness in a deeper way.

Let your heart rest in this today:

**You may feel alone, but you have never been abandoned.**

God is with you — and His presence fills every empty space with love.

# Chapter 5

# When You Feel Abandoned or Forgotten

**Isaiah 49:15–16**

*"Can a woman forget her nursing child, And not have compassion on the son of her womb? Surely they may forget, Yet I will not forget you.*
*See, I have inscribed you on the palms of My hands..."*

**Psalm 27:10**

*"When my father and my mother forsake me, Then the Lord will take care of me."*

**Deuteronomy 31:6**

*"...He will not leave you nor forsake you."*

**Joshua 1:9**

*"...for the Lord your God is with you wherever you go."*

**Psalm 139:7–10**

*"Where can I go from Your Spirit? Or where can I flee from Your presence?...*
*Even there Your hand shall lead me, And Your right hand shall hold me."*

## COMFORT FOR THE HEART

There are moments when being forgotten hurts deeply. When people leave, relationships fade, support disappears, and silence fills the places where love once lived.

But even in those moments, God's voice breaks through: **"I will not forget you."**

The Scriptures remind you of a healing truth:

People may forget you, **but God never does.**

People may walk away, **but God stays.**

People may overlook you, **but God sees you fully.**

He engraved your name on His hands— not lightly, not temporarily— but **permanently in love**.

That means you are: **Precious** to Him, **Remembered** by Him, **Held** by Him

Even the empty places inside you, God fills with His presence. Even the rejection you faced, He answers with acceptance.
Even when you felt invisible, He saw every tear and every quiet ache.

You may feel forgotten by people, but never by the One who created you.

Let your heart rest in this truth:

**God has not abandoned you.**
**He never left.**
**He never will.**

Where others let go, He holds you. Where others walk away, He walks beside you.

You are remembered. You are held. You are loved—
**deeply, endlessly, faithfully.**

# Section 2

## WHEN GOD BEGINS TO HEAL YOU

Healing doesn't always happen all at once. Here, you'll feel God's nearness, comfort, and gentle restoration as He begins to lift the weight from your heart.

# Chapter 6

# When God Draws Near to the Brokenhearted

**Psalm 34:18**

*"The Lord is near to those who have a broken heart, And saves such as have a contrite spirit."*

**Psalm 145:18**

*"The Lord is near to all who call upon Him..."*

**Isaiah 57:15**

*"...I dwell... with him who has a contrite and humble spirit, To revive the spirit of the humble, And to revive the heart of the contrite ones."*

**James 4:8**

*"Draw near to God and He will draw near to you."*

**Psalm 73:28**

*"But it is good for me to draw near to God..."*

**Lamentations 3:57**

*"You drew near on the day I called on You, And said, 'Do not fear!'"*

## COMFORT FOR THE HEART

There is a special closeness God gives to the brokenhearted — a nearness deeper than what most people ever experience.

Sometimes your heart breaks, and in the very same moment, you step into a level of God's presence you never knew before.

The Scriptures in this chapter reveal something precious:

**God does not wait for you to be strong before He comes near. He comes near *because* you are hurting.**

His nearness is not based on perfection, performance, or spiritual strength. It is based on His compassion. His tenderness. His understanding of your pain.

When your heart feels fragile, He comes close enough to revive it.

When tears fall silently, He sits beside you in the quiet.

When fear presses in, He whispers, "Do not fear."

He is not a distant God. He is not waiting at the finish line of your healing. He is walking every step with you.

The closer you draw to Him — even in whispered prayers — the closer He draws to you, bringing:

**peace, comfort, reassurance, strength, revival, rest**

And even when you don't feel Him, He is near — closer than your breath, holding your heart like something precious.

Let this truth settle into the deepest parts of you today:

**Your broken heart attracts the presence of God. Your pain does not push Him away — it draws Him in.**

You are not walking this valley alone. The God who loves you is near, and He is gently reviving your heart, one moment at a time.

# CHAPTER 7

# WHEN HIS COMFORT REACHES THE DEEP PLACES

**Corinthians 1:3–4**

*"The Father of mercies and God of all comfort, who comforts us in all our tribulation..."*

**Psalm 94:19**

*"In the multitude of my anxieties within me, Your comforts delight my soul."*

**Isaiah 66:13**

*"As one whom his mother comforts, So I will comfort you..."*

**Psalm 23:4**

*"Your rod and Your staff, they comfort me."*

**John 14:16**

*"And I will pray the Father, and He will give you another Helper, that He may abide with you forever."*

**Psalm 119:50**

*"This is my comfort in my affliction, For Your word has given me life."*

## COMFORT FOR THE HEART

There are places inside your heart that no one else can reach — places shaped by loss, disappointment, fear, or memories you rarely speak about.

But God reaches those places with a comfort no human could ever offer. The Scriptures in this chapter paint a beautiful picture of His tenderness:

He comforts *all* your tribulation. He brings delight to anxious thoughts. He comforts with the gentleness of a mother. He walks with you through the darkest valleys. He sends the Holy Spirit to abide with you forever. His Word breathes life where your heart feels faint.

His comfort isn't shallow. It doesn't sit on the surface of your pain. It goes deep — into the hidden places, the tucked-away emotions,
the quiet wounds you barely mention.

His comfort is not just something He gives — **comfort is part of who He is.**

He comes close not to judge your pain, but to heal it. Not to rush your healing, but to hold your heart while it recovers.

When His comfort reaches the deep places, something beautiful happens:

**fear softens, anxiety loosens, grief lifts, hope rises, your soul breathes again**

Let your heart rest in this truth:

**God's comfort isn't temporary — it is abiding, constant, and made exactly for your deepest needs.**

You are not beyond His healing.
You are not too broken for His comfort.
You are safe in His arms,
held in His presence,
and loved with a comfort that reaches all the way in.

# Chapter 8

# When He Begins Restoring What Was Lost

**Joel 2:25**

*"So I will restore to you the years that the swarming locust has eaten..."*

**Psalm 126:5–6**

*"Those who sow in tears, Shall reap in joy."*

**Jeremiah 30:17**

*"For I will restore health to you, and heal you of your wounds..."*

**1 Peter 5:10**

*"After you have suffered a while, ... the God of all grace... perfect, establish, strengthen, and settle you."*

**Isaiah 61:7**

*"Instead of your shame you shall have double honor... Therefore in their land they shall possess double; Everlasting joy shall be theirs."*

**Psalm 23:3**

*"He restores my soul..."*

## COMFORT FOR THE HEART

There are seasons when life feels like it has taken more than it has given. Years marked by loss, disappointment, broken relationships, missed opportunities, or deep wounds that changed the way you see yourself.

But restoration is not just something God *can* do. Restoration is something God **loves** to do.

The Scriptures in this chapter reveal a God who: restores the years you thought were wasted, brings joy out of seasons of tears, heals wounds you assumed were permanent, strengthens what became weak, replaces shame with honor, rebuilds the soul from the inside out.

Your loss does not intimidate Him. Your brokenness does not overwhelm Him. Your history does not limit His power.

If something was taken from you — a relationship, a season, a dream, a part of yourself — God knows how to restore it in a way that is better, deeper, richer, and stronger than before.

Restoration does not always look like going back to what was. Often, it looks like God giving you something **new**, something healed, something whole, something only He could create.

Let your heart rest in this promise today:

**Nothing you have lost is beyond God's ability to restore. Not a year, not a moment, not a part of your heart.**

He is already working behind the scenes, gathering what was scattered, healing what was wounded, rebuilding what fell apart.

Your story is not ending in loss — it is being rewritten with restoration. And joy is coming.

## Chapter 9

# When He Teaches Your Heart to Trust Again

**Proverbs 3:5–6**

*"Trust in the Lord with all your heart, And lean not on your own understanding; In all your ways acknowledge Him, And He shall direct your paths."*

**Psalm 56:3**

*"Whenever I am afraid, I will trust in You."*

**Isaiah 26:3**

*"You will keep him in perfect peace, Whose mind is stayed on You, Because he trusts in You."*

**Nahum 1:7**

*"The Lord is good, A stronghold in the day of trouble; And He knows those who trust in Him."*

**Jeremiah 17:7–8**

*"Blessed is the man who trusts in the Lord... He shall be like a tree planted by the waters..."*

## COMFORT FOR THE HEART

When your heart has been hurt, trust becomes one of the first things to fade and one of the last things to return.

Fear, disappointment, and past wounds whisper:

"Don't open your heart again."
"Don't expect anything good."
"You're safer staying guarded."

But the Scriptures you just read gently reveal another truth:

**God does not rush your trust — He rebuilds it.**

Trust isn't something He demands. Trust is something He *teaches*.

One small step at a time. One whisper of peace at a time. One moment of guidance at a time. And as He teaches your heart to trust again, He shows you:

His goodness, His faithfulness, His protection, His gentle leadership, His care over every detail.

You don't have to trust perfectly. You don't have to trust boldly. You don't have to trust without fear. You can trust Him right in the middle of your trembling. He meets you there.

When you lift your eyes, when you whisper a prayer, when you offer Him even a small part of your heart —

He receives it, He honors it, and He leads you with love.

Let this truth comfort you today:

**Trust grows not by forcing your heart, but by experiencing God's faithfulness — one moment at a time.**

He is patient with you. He is gentle with you. And He will guide you step by step until trusting Him becomes your peace again.

# Chapter 10

# When He Lifts the Weight of Sorrow

**Psalm 30:11**

*"You have turned for me my mourning into dancing; You have put off my sackcloth and clothed me with gladness."*

**Isaiah 61:3**

*"...to give them beauty for ashes, The oil of joy for mourning, The garment of praise for the spirit of heaviness..."*

**Psalm 55:22**

*"Cast your burden on the Lord, And He shall sustain you..."*

**Matthew 11:28**

*"Come to Me, all you who labor and are heavy laden, and I will give you rest."*

**1 Peter 5:7**

*"...casting all your care upon Him, for He cares for you."*

## COMFORT FOR THE HEART

Sorrow can feel like a weight — a heaviness that sits on the chest, follows you into every room, and makes even simple moments feel exhausting.

But God does not expect you to carry sorrow alone. He steps into your story and gently begins lifting the weight you were never meant to hold.

The Scriptures in this chapter show us a God who:

turns mourning into dancing, exchanges ashes for beauty, lifts heaviness and replaces it with praise, carries burdens that feel too heavy for your heart, gives rest to the weary and overwhelmed, takes every care because you matter to Him.

You may not feel the weight lift all at once. Sometimes the healing is gradual, like the slow rise of dawn after a long night.
Other times it happens in a moment —
a breath of peace,
a whisper of hope,
a sudden lightness in your spirit.

However He chooses to do it, one truth remains: **God is lifting the sorrow, not you.**

You don't have to force healing. You don't have to pretend you're strong. You simply come to Him — and He does the lifting.

Let your heart rest in this promise today:

**The weight you feel today is not permanent. God is already replacing it with joy, comfort, and renewed strength.**

Your mourning will become dancing. Your heaviness will become praise. Your sorrow will become gladness.

This is His heart for you — and He is faithful to complete what He started.

# Section 3

## WHEN HOPE STARTS TO RISE AGAIN

This is where the light begins to break through. Strength returns, courage awakens, and your heart starts to breathe again.

# Chapter 11

# When Your Heart Learns to Breathe Again

**Ezekiel 36:26**

*"I will give you a new heart and put a new spirit within you..."*

**Psalm 73:26**

*"My flesh and my heart fail; But God is the strength of my heart..."*

**Psalm 51:12**

*"Restore to me the joy of Your salvation, And uphold me by Your generous Spirit."*

**2 Corinthians 4:16**

*"Even though our outward man is perishing, yet the inward man is being renewed day by day."*

**John 20:22**

*"And when He had said this, He breathed on them, and said to them, 'Receive the Holy Spirit.'"*

## COMFORT FOR THE HEART

There comes a moment in healing when the heart quietly whispers: **"I think I'm going to be okay."**

It may not be loud. It may not feel strong. But it's there — a soft breath of hope returning after a long season of heaviness.

The Scriptures in this chapter celebrate that moment: God gives you a **new heart.** He renews your strength, He restores your joy, He revives your spirit day by day, His breath brings new life into weary places.

Healing doesn't always begin with a big breakthrough. Sometimes it begins with a single breath — a moment where sadness loosens, hope flickers, and your heart realizes it's not drowning anymore.

God is not just mending your heart; He is **reviving** it. Renewing it. Breathing life into places that once felt numb or tired.

Your heart is learning to breathe again because:

the weight is lifting

the darkness is thinning

the strength is returning

the Holy Spirit is moving

the joy is awakening

Let this truth fill your heart today:

**Healing doesn't erase your story —**
**it gives you breath to live again.**

You are rising.
You are healing.
You are breathing again —
and God is holding your heart every step of the way.

# Chapter 12

# When Hope Breaks Through the Darkness

**Psalm 30:5**

*"Weeping may endure for a night, But joy comes in the morning."*

**Isaiah 60:1**

*"Arise, shine; For your light has come! And the glory of the Lord is risen upon you."*

**Micah 7:8**

*"When I fall, I will arise; When I sit in darkness, The Lord will be a light to me."*

**John 1:5**

*"And the light shines in the darkness, and the darkness did not comprehend it."*

**Romans 15:13**

*"Now may the God of hope fill you with all joy and peace in believing..."*

## COMFORT FOR THE HEART

Dark seasons can feel endless. Nights feel long. Days feel heavy. The heart wonders if the light will ever return.

But hope has a way of breaking through when you least expect it — quietly, gently, but powerfully.

The Scriptures in this chapter remind you: Light always follows darkness. Joy is promised after weeping. The Lord Himself becomes your light. Darkness cannot overcome the light of Christ. Hope is something God *fills you with*, not something you must force.

Hope doesn't always burst through — sometimes it slips in like the first hint of sunrise, soft and slow, but undeniable.

The moment you feel even the smallest spark of hope, it's a sign that God is lifting you to a new place.

The darkness you've walked through is not your final destination. God is already illuminating the path ahead:

Where fear lived, peace is rising

Where sorrow sat, joy is awakening

Where heaviness lingered, light is breaking through

Let your heart embrace this truth:

**Darkness never wins against God's light. And His light is rising in you right now.**

You are stepping into a new day — not because the darkness suddenly left,
but because God stepped into the darkness with you
and brought His hope with Him.

The night is ending.
Morning is coming.
Hope is breaking through.

# CHAPTER 13

# WHEN GOD RENEWS YOUR STRENGTH

**Isaiah 40:31**

*"But those who wait on the Lord  Shall renew their strength;  They shall mount up with wings like eagles,  They shall run and not be weary,
They shall walk and not faint."*

**2 Corinthians 12:9**

*"My grace is sufficient for you, for My strength is made perfect in weakness."*

**Psalm 27:14**

*"Wait on the Lord;  Be of good courage,  And He shall strengthen your heart..."*

**Nehemiah 8:10**

*"...for the joy of the Lord is your strength."*

**Philippians 4:13**

*"I can do all things through Christ who strengthens me."*

## COMFORT FOR THE HEART

There are seasons when your strength feels completely gone — emotionally, physically, mentally, spiritually.

You try to push through, but everything feels heavy. Even simple tasks feel overwhelming. Your heart feels tired in a way sleep can't fix.

But the Scriptures in this chapter reveal something beautiful:

**God brings back the strength you thought you lost. He renews it, restores it, and fills you again.**

Strength doesn't return because you try harder. It returns because **He breathes it into you.**

God renews your strength by: lifting the heaviness, restoring joy, rebuilding courage, filling you with His power, meeting you in your weakness, sustaining you when you feel empty.

You may not feel like you're "flying like an eagle" yet — but even noticing the desire to rise is a sign that strength is returning.

You are not weak for feeling tired. You are not behind for feeling drained. You are not failing for needing rest.

You are human — and God delights in strengthening those who wait on Him. Let your heart hold onto this truth today:

**Your strength is not gone — it is being renewed.**

Every moment you wait on Him, lean on Him, cry out to Him, or simply breathe in His presence... He is pouring strength back into you.

And soon, very soon, you will run again. You will rise again. You will feel alive again.

Because the God who strengthens you never grows weary and never stops giving you the strength you need.

# Chapter 14

# When He Rebuilds Your Confidence

**Philippians 1:6**

*"...He who has begun a good work in you will complete it..."*

**Hebrews 10:35**

*"Therefore do not cast away your confidence,
which has great reward."*

**Psalm 27:1**

*"The Lord is my light and my salvation; Whom shall I fear?"*

**Proverbs 14:26**

*"In the fear of the Lord there is strong confidence..."*

**Isaiah 41:10**

*"Fear not, for I am with you... I will strengthen you, Yes, I will help you..."*

**2 Timothy 1:7**

*"For God has not given us a spirit of fear, but of power and of love and of a sound mind."*

## COMFORT FOR THE HEART

When your heart has been through deep hurt, confidence is often one of the first things to disappear.

You begin to doubt yourself — your choices, your voice, your worth, your ability to move forward.

But God is rebuilding your confidence — and He is doing it in a way that is gentle, steady, and sure.

The Scriptures in this chapter remind you: God finishes what He starts. Confidence has great reward. Fear loses its voice in His presence.

Trust in Him brings strong stability. He strengthens and helps you. You carry a spirit of power, love, and a sound mind

Your confidence is not returning because circumstances changed. It's returning because **God is changing you.**

He is restoring your sense of identity. He is reminding you of your worth. He is rebuilding the strength that was shaken. He is showing you that you are not walking forward alone.

Confidence doesn't come from pretending to be brave. It comes from knowing Who walks beside you and Who lives within you.

Let your heart rest in this truth today:

**You are not who the pain tried to make you. You are who God says you are — and He is rebuilding your confidence from the inside out.**

You can move forward.
You can speak again.
You can rise again.
You can trust your steps again.

Because the God who began a good work in you
is not finished —
and He never will be until you shine with the fullness of what He created you to be.

# Chapter 15

# When You Begin to See Light Again

**Psalm 112:4**

*"Unto the upright there arises light in the darkness; He is gracious, and full of compassion, and righteous."*

**Psalm 18:28**

*"For You will light my lamp; The Lord my God will enlighten my darkness."*

**Isaiah 58:10**

*"...then your light shall dawn in the darkness, And your darkness shall be as the noonday."*

**John 8:12**

*"I am the light of the world. He who follows Me shall not walk in darkness, but have the light of life."*

**Psalm 119:105**

*"Your word is a lamp to my feet and a light to my path."*

## COMFORT FOR THE HEART

There is a sacred moment in healing when you realize the darkness is no longer as heavy as it once was. It's not that everything is perfect — but something inside you has shifted. The light is returning.

Sometimes it begins with: a spark of hope, a moment of clarity, a breath of peace, or a simple awareness that things are not as dark as they were before.

The Scriptures in this chapter remind you: God lights your lamp. He brings dawn into your darkness. Jesus Himself is your Light. His Word guides your steps

You are no longer defined by darkness — you are light in Him

Light doesn't erase your memories, but it changes how you see them.

Light doesn't deny the pain, but it reveals the healing.

Light doesn't always come instantly, but once it begins to rise, nothing can stop it.

Your ability to see again —
to hope again,
to dream again,
to feel again —
is a sign that God has been working deeply in your heart.

Let this truth settle gently inside you today:

**The darkness you walked through is not where you're staying.**
**God's light is rising in you — and it will only grow brighter.**

You are stepping into clarity.
You are stepping into peace.
You are stepping into joy.
You are stepping into the light of His presence.

The night is passing.
The morning is arriving.
And your heart is waking up to the goodness of God again.

# Section 4

## WHEN JOY RETURNS TO YOUR HEART

Joy is your birthright. In this final section, God restores your joy, peace, and song — bringing your heart into a place of rejoicing again.

# Chapter 16

# When God Turns Your Tears Into Joy

**Psalm 30:11**

*"You have turned for me my mourning into dancing; You have put off my sackcloth and clothed me with gladness."*

**Psalm 126:5**

*"Those who sow in tears Shall reap in joy."*

**John 16:20**

*"...you will be sorrowful, but your sorrow will be turned into joy."*

**Jeremiah 31:13**

*"...I will turn their mourning into joy, Will comfort them, And make them rejoice rather than sorrow."*

**Psalm 5:11**

*"But let all those who put their trust in You rejoice..."*

**Nehemiah 8:10**

*"...for the joy of the Lord is your strength."*

## COMFORT FOR THE HEART

There is something sacred about every tear you have cried. None of them were pointless. None of them were unseen. None of them were forgotten by God.

Every tear had a purpose. Every tear watered the soil for the joy that is now beginning to grow.

The Scriptures in this chapter show us a God who: turns mourning into dancing, transforms sorrow into joy, replaces heaviness with gladness, comforts deeply, strengthens through joy, rewards trust with rejoicing.

Your tears were not a sign of weakness — they were a sign of your heart still fighting to heal.

And now, God is taking those same tears and turning them into the evidence of His goodness.

Joy doesn't always arrive loudly. Sometimes it begins as a gentle upward shift — a lightness in your spirit, a smile returning to your lips,
a sense of hope settling in your heart.

But once joy begins, it grows.

It grows because **God Himself is the One giving it to you.**
He is lifting the sorrow.
He is restoring gladness.
He is bringing back the beauty that pain tried to erase.

Let your heart rest in this truth today:

**Your tears were seeds.**
**Your joy is the harvest.**

God is turning your tears into joy —
and nothing can stop the joy He is bringing into your life.

# Chapter 17

# When He Fills You With His Peace Again

**John 14:27**

*"Peace I leave with you, My peace I give to you; not as the world gives do I give to you. Let not your heart be troubled, neither let it be afraid."*

**Philippians 4:7**

*"And the peace of God, which surpasses all understanding, will guard your hearts and minds through Christ Jesus."*

**Isaiah 26:3**

*"You will keep him in perfect peace, Whose mind is stayed on You, Because he trusts in You."*

**Colossians 3:15**

*"And let the peace of God rule in your hearts..."*

**Psalm 29:11**

*"The Lord will give strength to His people; The Lord will bless His people with peace."*

## COMFORT FOR THE HEART

Peace is not the absence of problems — it is the presence of God.

There are moments in life when peace feels far away… when your thoughts run fast, your emotions feel unsettled, and your heart feels restless.

But the Scriptures in this chapter remind you: **Peace is not something you must create — it is something Jesus *gives* you.**

He gives: a peace deeper than understanding, a peace that guards your heart, a peace that rules over anxious thoughts, a peace connected to His presence, a peace that remains even in storms

When peace leaves, it often feels sudden. But when peace returns, it settles slowly — softly — like calmness spreading across a still lake.

You begin to feel: steady again, grounded again, safe again, held again, hopeful again.

Not because circumstances changed, but because *He* is near.

His peace fills the places that once felt unsettled.
His peace replaces the fear that once controlled you.
His peace anchors you when emotions try to rise again.

Let your heart hold onto this truth today:

**Peace is not lost — it is returning. He is giving it to you, moment by moment, breath by breath.**

And as His peace fills you, you will feel the weight lift, the fear quiet, and the joy grow.

You are held by the Prince of Peace — and His peace is filling your heart again.

# Chapter 18

# When He Restores Your Song

**Psalm 40:3**

*"He has put a new song in my mouth— Praise to our God..."*

**Psalm 96:1**

*"Oh, sing to the Lord a new song! Sing to the Lord, all the earth."*

**Psalm 71:23**

*"My lips shall greatly rejoice when I sing to You, And my soul, which You have redeemed."*

**Isaiah 51:11**

*"...Everlasting joy shall be upon their heads; They shall obtain joy and gladness; Sorrow and sighing shall flee away."*

**Psalm 98:4**

*"Shout joyfully to the Lord, all the earth; Break forth in song, rejoice, and sing praises."*

**Ephesians 5:19**

*"...singing and making melody in your heart to the Lord."*

## COMFORT FOR THE HEART

There are seasons when you lose your "song" — not just music, but the joy, hope, and worship that once flowed naturally from your heart.

Pain can silence you. Loss can quiet you. Fear can steal your voice. Grief can make it hard to rejoice. But the beautiful truth is this:

**God restores what pain tried to silence.**

The Scriptures in this chapter reveal a God who: puts a *new* song in your mouth, fills your heart with rejoicing, replaces sighing with gladness, causes sorrow to flee, fills your soul with melody again.

Your new song doesn't have to sound like your old one. Sometimes it's softer. Sometimes it's deeper. Sometimes it's born from the very places you once cried.

But it is real. It is pure. It is worship that flows from a healed heart.

Your song returning is a sign of: hope restored, joy awakened, peace returning, gratitude alive again, God's faithfulness proven.

Let your heart rest in this truth today:

**The same God who caught your tears is now restoring your song.**

Your worship is returning. Your joy is rising. Your voice is awakening. Your heart is singing again — not because life is perfect, but because God has been faithful.

And the song He gives you now will be one of the most beautiful worships of your life.

# Chapter 19

# When You Feel His Goodness Surrounding You

**Psalm 23:6**

*"Surely goodness and mercy shall follow me All the days of my life..."*

**Psalm 31:19**

*"Oh, how great is Your goodness, Which You have laid up for those who fear You..."*

**Nahum 1:7**

*"The Lord is good, A stronghold in the day of trouble..."*

**Psalm 145:9**

*"The Lord is good to all, And His tender mercies are over all His works."*

**Romans 8:28**

*"And we know that all things work together for good to those who love God..."*

**Psalm 27:13**

*"I would have lost heart, unless I had believed that I would see the goodness of the Lord in the land of the living."*

## COMFORT FOR THE HEART

There is a moment in healing when your heart becomes aware of something beautiful:

**God's goodness has been surrounding you the entire time — even in the moments you couldn't feel it.**

His goodness didn't begin when the pain ended. It didn't wait for the valley to pass. It didn't arrive only when things improved.

His goodness has been: following you, covering you, carrying you, strengthening you, healing you, guiding you, sustaining you.

Even in the tears, even in the silence, even in the confusion, even in the waiting, even in the heartbreak.

The Scriptures in this chapter remind you: His goodness is stored up for you. His goodness is with you in trouble. His goodness is for *everyone* — including you. His goodness works all things together for good. His goodness will be seen **in your lifetime.**

Pain might have tried to convince you that you were alone, but His goodness has been your constant companion.

Now, your heart is awakening to it. You're beginning to recognize: the peace He gave you, the strength He restored, the hope He rekindled, the joy He returned, the healing He performed quietly and faithfully.

Let your heart rest in this truth today:

**You are surrounded — absolutely wrapped — in the goodness of God.**

His goodness is behind you, before you, beside you, over you, and within you.

And as you breathe it in, you will find your heart overflowing with gratitude and joy.

# Chapter 20

# When Your Heart Rejoices Again

**Psalm 28:7**

*"The Lord is my strength and my shield; My heart trusted in Him, and I am helped; Therefore my heart greatly rejoices, And with my song I will praise Him."*

**Psalm 118:24**

*"This is the day the Lord has made; We will rejoice and be glad in it."*

**Psalm 16:11**

*"In Your presence is fullness of joy; At Your right hand are pleasures forevermore."*

**Isaiah 55:12**

*"For you shall go out with joy, And be led out with peace..."*

**Philippians 4:4**

*"Rejoice in the Lord always. Again I will say, rejoice!"*

## COMFORT FOR THE HEART

There is nothing quite like the moment your heart realizes: **"I am joyful again."**

It doesn't mean every circumstance is perfect. It doesn't mean the past has been erased. It doesn't mean you'll never cry again.

It means something better: **God has restored your joy. Your heart is alive again. Your spirit has risen again.**

The Scriptures in this chapter show the beautiful fullness of this truth: God became your strength. He shielded your heart. He helped you through every valley. Joy returned because He was with you. His presence filled you with gladness. Peace accompanies your steps. Worship rises naturally from within you.

This is not the kind of joy the world gives. This is the joy that comes from: surviving the storm, being held in your weakness, experiencing His comfort, watching hope rise, feeling light return, seeing His goodness surround you, and realizing... He never left you.

Your rejoicing is a testimony: "I made it through with God. My heart is no longer broken — it's whole, strengthened, and singing again."

Let your heart embrace this truth today: **Your joy is not fragile. Your joy is restored by God — and what He restores, He protects.**

This is the joy that carries you into the next chapter of your life, the joy that fuels your worship, and the joy that reminds you: **God has been faithful. God has healed you. And God has brought your heart back to life.**

Your heart rejoices again — and this is only the beginning.

# Declarations for a Healed Heart

Speak these out loud.
Let them settle into your spirit.

God is healing me, and I receive His peace.

My heart is growing stronger day by day.

I am deeply loved, and I am never alone.

God is restoring what I lost.

Hope is rising in me again.

Joy is mine, and I will walk in it.

My mind is steady, my heart is whole, and my spirit is secure in Him.

My future is held safely in God's hands.

# Reflection Questions

## A Place for Your Heart to Respond

### Looking Back at Your Healing Journey

Which chapter spoke most deeply to your heart? Why?

What part of your heart did God begin to heal as you read?

How has your understanding of God's love and nearness changed?

What moments of hope did you feel rising again?

Where have you seen God's goodness show up recently?

### Moving Forward in Strength & Joy

What burdens is God asking you to release?

Which Scriptures from this book will you carry into your next season?

What does "joy returning" look like for you personally?

What step of healing or faith can you take this week?

What is your heartfelt prayer today?

# My Personal Prayer for You

Father,
I lift up the precious reader holding this book.
Thank You for meeting them on every page
and touching the deep places of their heart.

Surround them with Your peace.
Strengthen them with Your joy.
Wrap them in Your love.
Heal every wound — seen and unseen.

Let hope rise within them like the morning light.
Let Your presence steady their steps.
Let Your goodness overwhelm their life.

Guide them into every promise You have spoken
and let their heart rejoice in You more and more each day.

In Jesus' name,

Amen.

# Final Encouragement

**A Final Word for Your Heart**

As you close this book, I want you to pause and notice something sacred:

**You are not the same person you were when you began.**

You have walked through pages that touched deep places in your heart. You have given God room to speak, to comfort, to strengthen, and to breathe life back into you.

You have allowed Him to meet you in your pain, to hold you in the heaviness, to lift your sorrow, and to restore your joy.

Please don't rush past this moment.

Take a breath and recognize:

Hope has risen.

Your heart is lighter.

Peace is settling.

Joy is awakening.

God is near — closer than ever.

Healing isn't about being perfect or never hurting again. It's about walking with the One who never leaves, never fails, and never stops loving you.

So if you ever feel discouraged again, come back to these pages.
Read them slowly.
Let the Word wash over you.
Let the God who healed you continue to heal you.

**Your journey is not ending — you are stepping into a new chapter of strength, hope, and joy.**

You are loved.
You are held.
You are healing.
And you are never, ever alone.

# Closing Blessing

May the God who sees every tear and knows every ache wrap His arms around your heart and continue the healing He has begun in you.

May His peace settle over your mind, quieting every storm and calming every anxious thought.

May His joy return to you in unexpected moments — a smile you didn't plan, a lightness you didn't expect, a hope that rises gently inside your chest.

May His presence be your comfort, His Word be your strength, and His love be the anchor that holds you steady through every season.

May you feel Him walking beside you, before you, behind you, and within you — whispering, "You are Mine, you are loved, and you are never alone."

As you move forward, may your heart grow stronger, your faith grow deeper, your joy grow fuller, and your life reflect the healing work He has lovingly performed.

This is not the end of your story — this is the beginning of a restored, renewed, joy-filled chapter of your life.

**May your heart continue to heal, continue to rise, and continue to rejoice in the God who holds you so tenderly.**

**Amen.**

# About the Author

Cindy August is an Author, Guest Speaker, Teacher, and Minister of the Gospel of Jesus Christ through songs expressed in Sign Language and flags.

She is the founder of Creative Books Plus Publishing and a faith-based writer devoted to helping others grow in their walk with God through inspiration, creativity, and grace.

Cindy is the author of *Signing for Worship, Words of Wisdom, My Life Story for My Grandchild: A Fill-In Journal,* and numerous devotional and low-content books that encourage reflection and spiritual growth.

She also co-authored two works with her father, George E. Boyer — *Flight of the Flyaways and Kold Stanton Kourage.*

Cindy and her husband, Don, live in North Carolina, and together they have two sons, two daughters, thirteen grandchildren, and five great-grandchildren.

www.ingramcontent.com/pod-product-compliance
Lightning Source LLC
LaVergne TN
LVHW010943110826
845149LV00013B/2734

* 9 7 8 1 9 7 0 9 4 7 0 7 6 *